Ray Charles

A MAN AND HIS SOUL

Copyright © 1986 by CPP/BELWIN, INC.
15800 N.W. 48th Avenue, Miami, Florida 33014
Art: Adriane Pirro / Editor: David C. Olsen / ISBN: 0-89898-500-5

RAY CHARLES has the distinction of being both a national treasure and an international phenomenon.

He started out from nowhere; years later finds him a global entity.

Hundreds of thousands of fingers have hit typewriter and word processor keyboards telling and retelling his story because it is uniquely American, an examplar of what we like to think is the best in us and our way of life.

The Ray Charles story is full of paradoxes, part and parcel of the American Dream.

Rags to riches. Triumph overcoming tragedy. Light transcending darkness.

The name Ray Charles is on a Star on Hollywood Boulevard's Walk of Fame. His bronze bust is enshrined in the Playboy Hall of Fame. There is the bronze medallion cast and presented to him by the French Republic on behalf of its people. There are the Halls of Fame: Rhythm & Blues, Jazz, Rock & Roll. There are the many gold records and the 10 Grammys.

There is the blackness and the blindness. There was the extreme poverty; there was the segregated South into which he was born.

It is music, Ray Charles' single driving force, that catapulted a poor, black, blind, orphaned teenager from there to here.

> "I was born with music inside me. That's the only explanation I know of ..." he remarks in his autobiography

> "Music was one of my parts. ...Like my blood. It was a force already with me when I arrived on the scene. It was a necessity for me — like food or water.

> "Music is nothing separate from me. It is me. ...You'd have to remove the music surgically."

Ray Charles Robinson was not born blind, only poor.

The first child of Aretha and Bailey Robinson was born in Albany, Ga, on September 23, 1930.

He hit the road early, at about three months, when the Robinsons moved across the border to Greenville, FL. It was the height of the Depression years. And the Robinsons had started out poor.

> "You hear folks talking about being poor." Charler recounts. "Even compared to other blacks... we were on the bottom of the ladder looking up at everyone else. Nothing below us except the ground."

It took three years, starting when Ray Charles was four, for the country boy who loved to look at the blazing sun at its height, the boy who loved to try to catch lightning, the boy who loved to strike matches to see their fierce, brief glare, to travel the path from light to darkness.

But Ray Charles has almost seven years of sight memory — colors, the things of backwoods country, and the face of the most important person in his early life: his mother, Aretha Robinson.

St. Augustine's was the Florida state school for the deaf and blind. Ray Charles was accepted as a charity student.

He learned to Braille and to type. He became a skilled basket weaver. He was allowed to develop his great gift of music.

He discovered mathematics and its correlation to music. He learned to compose and arrange music in his head, telling out the parts, one by one.

He remained at St. Augustine's until his mother's death when he set out "on the road again" for the first time as a struggling professional musician.

The road to greatness was no picnic, proverbial or literal. In fact, while earning his dues around and about Florida, he almost starved at times, hanging out at various Musicians' Locals, picking up gigs when he could.

He began to build himself a solo act, imitating Nat "King" Cole. When he knew it was time to head on, he asked a friend to find him the farthest point from Florida on a map of the continental U.S.

Seattle, WA. For Ray Charles, the turning point.

In Seattle he became a minor celebrity in local clubs. There he met an even younger musician, Quincy Jones, whom he took under his wing, marking the beginning of an intertwining of two musical lifetimes.

It was from Seattle that he went to Los Angeles to cut his first professional recording. And it was in Seattle, with Gossady McGee, that he formed the McSon Trio — Robin (son) and (Mc) Gee — in 1948, the first black group to have a sponsored TV show in the Pacific Northwest.

Along the way he'd shortened his name in deference to the success of "Sugar" Ray Robinson.

As Ray Charles he toured for about a year with Lowell Fulsom's band. He formed a group and played with singer Ruth Brown. He played the Apollo, the landmark showcase for black talent. He aspired to Carnegie Hall, then as now epitomizing the pinnacle of artistic success.

These were also the years that brought Charles the first band of his own, his first big hit record, "I Got A Woman."

By the early 1960's Ray Charles had accomplished his dream. He'd come of age musically. He had become a great musician, posting musical milestones along his route.

He'd made it to Carnegie Hall. The hit records ("Georgia," "Born to Lose") successively kept climbing to the top of the charts. He'd made his first triumphant European concert tour in 1960 (a feat which, except for 1965, he's repeated at least once a year ever since).

He'd treated himself to the formation of his first big band in 1961. In 1962, together with his long-time friend and personal manager, Joe Adams, he oversaw construction of his own office building and recording studio in Los Angeles, RPM International.

He had taken virtually every form of popular music and broken through its boundaries with such awe-inspiring achievements as the LP's "Genius Plus Soul Equals Jazz" and "Modern Sounds in Country & Western."

Rhythm & blues (or "race music" as it had been called) became universally respectable through his efforts. Jazz found a mainstream audience it had never previously enjoyed. And country & western music began to chart an unexpected course to general acceptance, then worldwide popularity. Along the way Ray Charles was instrumental in the invention of rock & roll.

His music is still marked by the unpredictability that is the genius of consummate artistry.

He is master of his soul, musically and personally.

To this day he selects and produces his own recording material with utter disregard for trends. He doesn't find the time nor necessity to write as much as he once did, but what he gleans, "from the attic of my mind," either old or new, is inevitably surprising, unique, "right."

In the past decade he has taken on George Gershwin ("Porgy and Bess"), Rodgers and Hammerstein ("Some Enchanted Evening," "Oh What a Beautiful Morning") and "America the Beautiful" — all with resounding, if unexpected, success.

Despite his intense reticence to expose the personal portion of his life to public scrutiny, Ray Charles is as outspoken about his opinions on matters of global interest as he is about matters of music.

As a Southern black, segregation was Ray Charles' dubious birthright. But racial tension and friction were not a part of his early rural years. At St. Augustine's the rules of segregation were strictly adhered to, both for the deaf and the blind children, a fact that even young Ray Charles found ironic.

"I knew being blind was suddenly an aid. I never learned to stop at the skin. If I looked at a man or a woman, I wanted to see inside. Being distracted by shading or coloring is stupid. It gets in the way. It's something I just can't see."

It was on the road in the 1950's that the realities of segregation, its evils, its injustices, even its ludicrous moments, became apparent to Charles and his troupe of traveling musicians.

It was a concert date in Augusta, GA that brought the issue of segregation vs. civil rights to a head for Ray Charles.

> "A promoter insisted that a date we were about to play be segregated: the blacks upstairs and the whites downstairs."

> "I told the promoter that I didn't mind segregation, except that he had it backwards... After all, I was black and it only made sense to have the black folk close to me... Let him sue. I wasn't going to play. And I didn't. And he sued. And I lost."

This was the incident that propelled Ray Charles into an active role in the quest for racial justice, the development of social consciousness that led him to friendship with moral and financial support of the Rev. Martin Luther King, Jr. in the 1960's.

> "... early on, I decided that if I was going to shoot craps on anyone's philosophy, I was putting my money on Martin Luther King, Jr."

> "I figured if I was going to pick up my cross and follow someone, it could only be Martin."

Despite his deep commitment to King and the cause of black Americans, Charles came to the logical conclusion that there was no place for him physically in the front lines:

> "First, I wouldn't have known when to duck when they started throwing broken bottles at my head. And I told that to Martin personally.

> "When he intentionally broke the law, he was hauled off to jail. And when you go to jail, you need money for lawyers, for legal research, for court fees, for food for the marchers. I saw that as my function; I helped raise money."

His awareness of racial injustice was not limited to the home front: The same years he fought the war against racial injustice in the American South found in Charles a growing awareness of racial injustice abroad, particularly the notorious policy of apartheid in South Africa.

Uniformed anti-apartheid groups have occasionally questioned Charles' 1981 concert appearances there.

> "It burns me up," he retorts acidly, "because people should've checked my record on civil rights before they opened their mouths.

> "How can anyone tell me where I can play my music? I went to South Africa because people — black and white — wanted to hear me.

> And it was in my contracts that the blacks wouldn't be seated in the rear."

Charles' manager, Joe Adams, himself black, further sets the record straight:

> "In the late 1970's, our office received a number of requests from several of the new Black Nations of South Africa for Ray Charles to come and perform. These requests were answered in 1981 when he made numerous appearances for these black nations. This tour represented the first totally integrated audiences in such major cities as Johannesburg and Capetown. He was approached to play Sun City for a huge fee. Instead he chose to play before totally black or integrated audiences with a fully integrated show.

> "As now, the orchestra consisted at the time of Asians, Latins, Caucasians, and blacks, all of whom performed together on the same stages, traveled together on the same buses, and stayed at the same hotels — an unheard of feat in South Africa and one that could have brought severe penalties to all concerned."

Modes to the point of mum about his humanitarian and charitable activities, Ray Charles makes an exception for the State of Israel and world Jewry.

Among the many, the world leader Charles has most enjoyed meeting is David Ben-Gurion, with whom he had a conversation of many hours during a concert tour of Israel not long before Ben-Gurion's death.

And the award among the hundreds he claims to have touched him most is the Beverly Hills Lodge of the B'nai Brith's tribute to him as its "Man of the Year" in 1976.

> "Even though I'm not Jewish," he explains, "and even though I'm stingy with my bread, Israel is one of the few causes I feel good about supporting.

> "Blacks and Jews are hooked up and bound together by a common history of persecution...

> "If someone besides a black ever sings the real gut bucket blues, it'll be a Jew. We both know what it's like to be someone else's footstool."

It all comes back to music, so inseparable from Ray Charles.

He keeps rolling along, doing what he does uniquely and wondrously well.

Ray Charles is a national treasure and a global phenomenon for this obvious reason: He is a master of his soul; he is music; he is himself.

GEORGIA ON MY MIND

Words by
STUART GORRELL

Music by
HOAGY CARMICHAEL

Georgia On My Mind - 3 - 1

I CAN'T STOP LOVING YOU

By
DON GIBSON

I Can't Stop Loving You - 2 - 1

WHAT'D I SAY

Words and Music by
RAY CHARLES

SWANEE RIVER ROCK

Words and Music by
RAY CHARLES

Swanee River Rock - 3 - 1

Swanee River Rock - 3 - 2

RUBY

Words by
MITCHELL PARISH

Music by
HEINZ ROEMHELD

They say, Ru - by, you're like a dream, not al - ways what you seem, _____ and tho' my heart may break when I a - wake, ___ let it be so, ___ I on - ly know, Ru - by, it's you. _____ They

Ruby - 3 - 1

ONE MINT JULEP

Words and Music by
RUDOLPH TOOMBS

Slow Rock

One Mint Julep - 3 - 1

One Mint Julep - 3 - 2

One Mint Julep - 3 - 3

HIT THE ROAD JACK

Words and Music by
PERCY MAYFIELD

Moderate beat

Hit the road Jack and don't you come back no more, no more, no more, no more. Hit the

road Jack and don't you come back no more._____ Hit the

more._____ Woo! Wom-an, oh wom-an, don't treat me so mean, You're the

Hit The Road Jack - 3 - 1

YOU ARE MY SUNSHINE

Words and Music by
JIMMIE DAVIS and
CHARLES MITCHELL

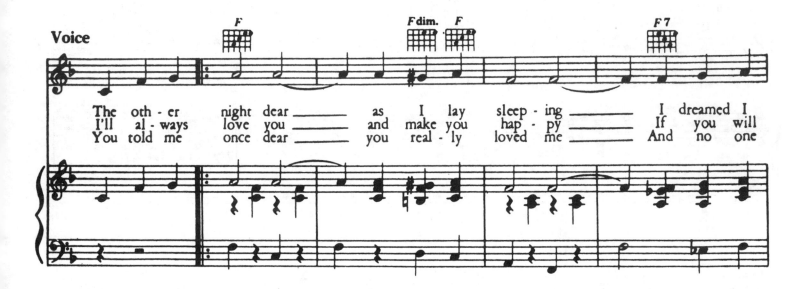

The oth-er night dear _____ as I lay sleep-ing _____ I dreamed I
I'll al-ways love you _____ and make you hap-py _____ If you will
You told me once dear _____ you real-ly loved me _____ And no one

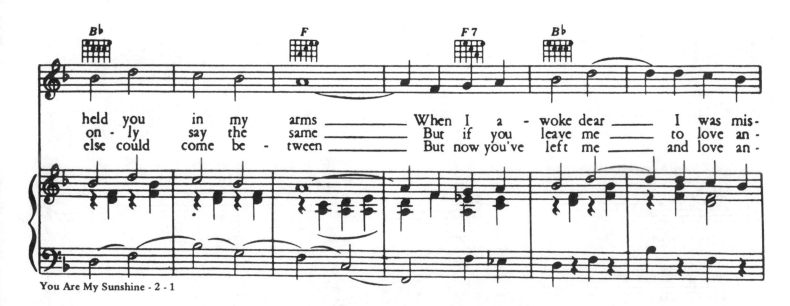

held you in my arms _____ When I a-woke dear _____ I was mis-
on-ly say the same _____ But if you leave me _____ to love an-
else could come be-tween _____ But now you've left me _____ and love an-

You Are My Sunshine - 2 - 1

You Are My Sunshine - 2 - 2

TAKE THESE CHAINS FROM MY HEART

By
FRED ROSE and
HY HEATH

Take These Chains From My Heart - 2 - 1

Take These Chains From My Heart - 2 - 2

THAT LUCKY OLD SUN
(Just Rolls Around Heaven All Day)

Words by
HAVEN GILLESPIE

Music by
BEASLEY SMITH

That Lucky Old Sun - 2 - 1

That Lucky Old Sun - 2 - 2

YOU DON'T KNOW ME

Words and Music by
CINDY WALKER &
EDDY ARNOLD

You Don't Know Me - 3 - 1

know the one — who dreams of you at night and longs to kiss your lips — and longs to hold you tight. — To you I'm just a friend, — that's all I've ev- er been, — but you don't know me. — For I — nev-er knew the art of mak-ing love, though my heart ached with love for you. — A -

DON'T CHANGE ON ME

Words and Music by
EDDIE REEVES and
JIMMY HOLIDAY

Verse — Medium beat

1. Girl, you're my sun-shine, you chase a-way the rain-drops,__ make it all__ worth-while.__ Make all the pain stop, just like a riv - er, Keep love__ flow - in' don't let our world stop, keep it go - in'. Oh, I

Chorus

like you just the way you are,__ hon - ey, Don't Change On Me,__ Don't Change On me,__ please Don't Change__ On Me.__ Girl, you're my luck - y star,__ hon - ey, Don't

Don't Change On Me - 3 - 1

IN THE HEAT OF THE NIGHT

Words by
MARILYN and ALAN BERGMAN

Music by
QUINCY JONES

In The Heat ___ Of The Night, ___

seems like a cold sweat creep-in' 'cross my brow. ___

In The Heat ___ Of The Night, ___ I'm feel-ing moth-er-less some-

how. ___ Stars ___ with e-vil eyes ___ stare from the

In The Heat Of The Night - 3 - 1

skies,_____ all mean and bright. *(In The Heat Of The Night)* Ain't a wo-man__ yet been

born,_____ knows how to make the morn-in' come._____

So hard_____ to keep con-trol,_____ when I'd sell my

soul_____...for just a lit-tle light! *(In The Heat Of The Night)* In The Heat__ Of The

UNDERSTANDING
(Is The Best Thing In The World)

Words and Music by
JIMMY HOLIDAY and
RAY CHARLES

Understanding - 3 - 1

44

(Spoken)

1. You know what I mean and it hurts me to see some
2. And she understands that a man's got to have respect

of my friends floundering thru' their life, never knowing the
What I mean is that if she must play around, don't let me

meaning of the word understanding. For instance,
catch her, 'cause it's a well known fact, that what a man don't

Me and my woman, we got a good thing going because of
see don't hurt him. You dig? Now listen, On the other hand;

BORN TO LOSE

Words and Music by
TED DAFFAN

Born To Lose - 2 - 1

CRYING TIME

Words and Music by
BUCK OWENS

Oh, it's cry-ing time a-gain, you're gon-na leave me; I can
say that ab-sence makes the heart grow fond-er, And that

see that far-a-way look in your eyes. I can tell, by the
tears are on-ly rain, to make love grow. Well, my love for you could

way you held me, dar-ling, That it won't be long be-
nev-er grow no strong-er, If I live to be a

Crying Time - 2 - 1

NO ONE

Words and Music by
DOC POMUS and
MORT SHUMAN

No One - 2 - 1

A BIT OF SOUL

Words and Music by
RAY CHARLES

A Bit Of Soul - 2 - 1

A Bit Of Soul - 2 - 2

LET THE GOOD TIMES ROLL

Words and Music by
LEONARD LEE

1. Come on, ba-by, LET THE GOOD TIMES ROLL,__ Come on, ba-by, let me thrill your soul;
2. Come on, ba-by, gon-na have a ball,__ Put our trou-bles up a-gainst the wall;

Come on,__ ba-by, LET THE GOOD TIMES ROLL,__ Roll on and on.__

1. Come on, ba-by, let me hold you tight,__ Tell me ev-'ry-thing is right to-night;
2. Come on, ba-by, let us paint the town,__ Don't let noth-in' ev-er bring us down;
(Opt.) 3. Let's go, ba-by, on a cra-zy fling,__ Love can be__ such a swing-in' thing;

Let The Good Times Roll - 2 - 1

Let The Good Times Roll - 2 - 2

COME LIVE WITH ME

Words and Music by
BOUDLEAUX and
FELICE BRYANT

Come Live With Me - 3 - 1

58

Come Live With Me - 3 - 3

LIVING FOR THE CITY

Words and Music by
STEVIE WONDER

1. A boy is born_____ in Hard-time, Mis - sis - sip - pi,
2. His fa - ther works_____ some days for four - teen ho - urs

sur - round - ed by_____ four walls that ain't so pret - ty._____ His par - ents give_____ him
and you can bet_____ he bare - ly makes a dol - lar._____ His mo - ther goes_____ to scrub

Living For The City - 3 - 1

3. His sister's black but she is sho'nuff pretty.
   Her skirt is short but Lord her legs are sturdy to walk to school.
   She's got to get up early, her clothes are old; but never are they dirty.
   Living just enough, just enough for the city.

4. Her brother's smart, he's got more sense than many.
   His patience's long but soon he won't have any. To find a job
   Is like a haystack needle, 'cause where he lives they don't
   Use colored people. Living just enough, just enough for the city.

HALLELUJAH I LOVE HER SO

Words and Music by
RAY CHARLES

Let me tell you 'bout a boy I know. (girl) He is my ba-by and he (She) lives next door. Ev-'ry morn-ing 'fore the sun comes up, He brings my cof-fee in my fav-'rite cup. That's why I know, yes, I

Hallelujah I Love Her So - 4 - 1

*Make knocking sound

Hallelujah I Love Her So - 4 - 3

Hallelujah I Love Her So - 4 - 4

A PERFECT LOVE

Words and Music by
PAUL WILLIAMS

A Perfect Love - 5 - 1

love that's al-ways new   Yes I   owe it all   to you 'cause when the

world out-side was sure that I was   on - ly chas-ing rain-bows

you could find   the words to make me   strong   Hold-ing

on   to me   and whis--per-ing "There's noth-ing wrong with rain-bows"   you

A Perfect Love - 5 - 4

time for me to go　　　and it would　help me just　to know that you'd re-

mem-ber me　as one who　came to　love　　　and found　A

Per - fect Love　to help a - long　the　way.

SHAKE YOUR TAIL FEATHERS

Words and Music by
RUDY LOVE, PEGGY LOVE, DIANNE LOVE, DENISE LOVE,
GERALD LOVE, TYREE JUDY & ZEBEDED PHILLIPS

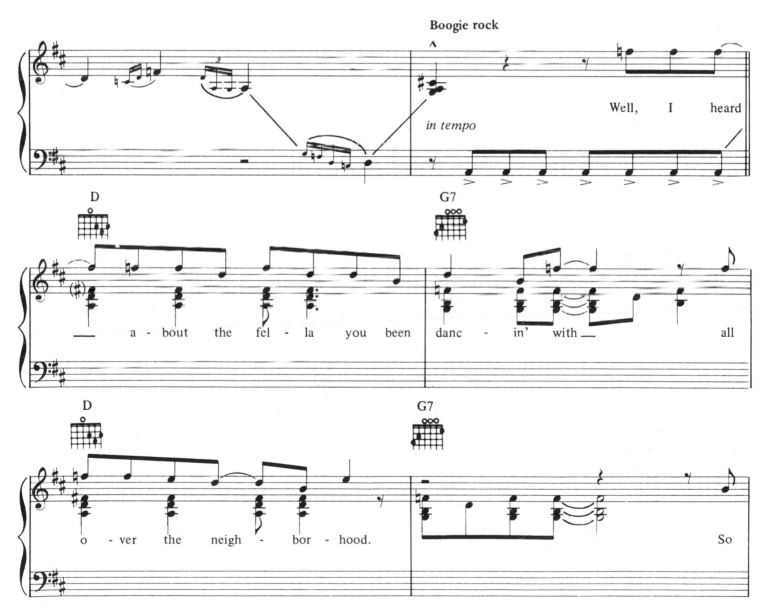

Shake Your Tail Feathers - 5 - 1

Shake Your Tail Feathers - 5 - 3

see you shake your tail - feath-er, Come on ___ and let me see you shakeyour tail - feath-er.

vocal gliss.

D   G7

Come on, come on, baby. Come on, baby, Yeah, come on babe. Do the twist, Do the frog, Do the swim, boogaloo? Ow, the bony moronie. Do the twist etc.

D   G7

Repeat for vocal improvisations
Then D.S. and fade %

And do the bird. Hey watusi, And what about the frug; Do the mashed potato, what about the

IT AIN'T GONNA WORRY MY MIND

By
RICHARD LEIGH

It Ain't Gonna Worry My Mind - 2 - 1

Verse 2:
Got no money in my pocket;
You don't get rich working over-time.
But long as you can't buy springtime in Virginia,
It ain't gonna worry, it ain't gonna worry,
It ain't gonna worry my mind.

Verse 3:
So go on wishin', go on prayin'.
Go on sayin', I'll hit better times.
But how in the world could she love me any better?
It ain't gonna worry, it ain't gonna worry,
It ain't gonna worry my mind.

It Ain't Gonna Worry My Mind - 2 - 2

BABY GRAND

Words and Music by
BILLY JOEL

Baby Grand - 6 - 1

keep ___ those mem-o-ries hold-ing on. ___

8va bassa- - - - - - - -

I've come far from the life I strayed in;

I've got scars from those dives I played in.

Now I'm home, and I'm wea-ry ___

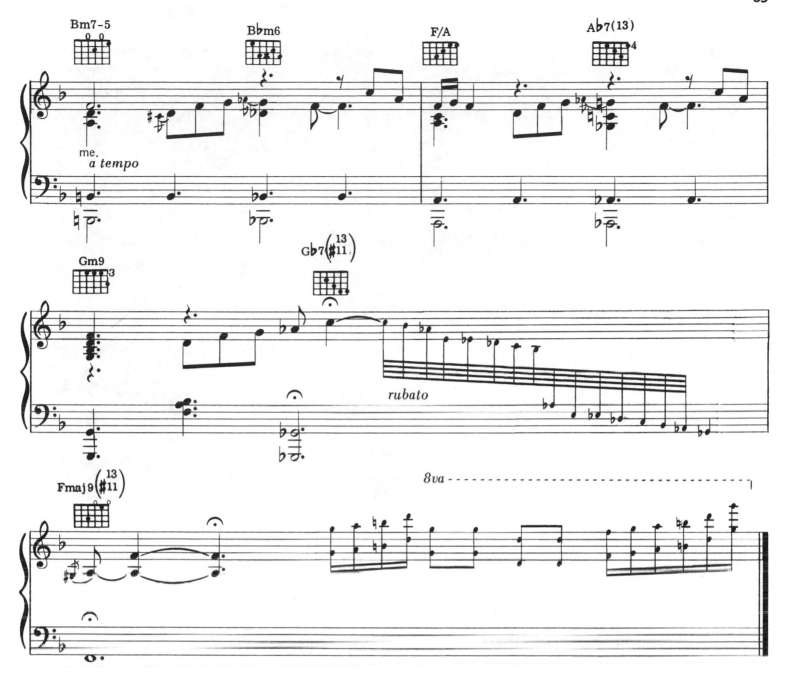

Verse 2:
In my time, I've wandered everywhere
Around this world; she would always be there,
Any day, any hour;
All it takes is the power in my hands.
This baby grand's been good to me.

Verse 3:
I've had friends, but they slipped away.
I've had fame, but it doesn't stay.
I've made fortunes, spent them fast enough.
As for women, they don't last with just one man;
But Baby Grand will stand by me.

(To Bridge:)

Billy Joel with Ray Charles

PHOTO: Sam Emerson

Mickey Gilley with Ray Charles

photo credit: RON KEITH